Does the Reformation Still Matter?

CALVIN SHORTS

A series published by the Calvin College Press

Does the Reformation Still Matter?

by Karin Maag

CALVIN SHORTS

Calvin COLLEGE PRESS

Grand Rapids, MI • calvincollegepress.com

Published 2016 by the Calvin College Press
3201 Burton St. SE
Grand Rapids, MI 49546

Publisher's Cataloging-in-Publication data
Names: Maag, Karin, author.
Title: Does the Reformation still matter today? / by Karin Maag.
Series: Calvin Shorts.
Description: Includes bibliographical references. | Grand Rapids, MI: Calvin College Press, 2016.
Identifiers: ISBN 978-1-937555-23-8 (pbk.) | 978-1-937555-24-5 (ebook) | LCCN 2016958541
Subjects: LCSH Reformation. | Church history. | BISAC Religion/Christian Church/History | Religion/Christianity/Protestant
Classification: LCC BR141 .M33 2016 | DCC 270--dc23

Cover design: Robert Alderink
Interior design and typeset: Katherine Lloyd, The DESK

Contents

Acknowledgements

I want to thank Susan Felch, executive editor of the Calvin Shorts series, for her confidence in me and her willingness to consider my essay for the series. I am deeply grateful to the Calvin Institute of Christian Worship for their underwriting of this publication. Thanks also to Dale Williams for all his work, particularly in developing the concept for the book cover. Pennylyn Dykstra-Pruim and Suzanne MacDonald served as reviewers, and their feedback was immensely helpful, as was that of Paul Fields, the Meeter Center curator. Calvin College students Kielley Lemkuil and Kellie Martin read through the manuscript in July 2016, testing out its readability, and made good suggestions. I am also deeply grateful to Laura Beer, the Meeter Center program coordinator, who carefully read through the entire manuscript, provided cogent feedback, and helped with the glossary.

This work is dedicated with respect and admiration to the senior citizens who have attended my classes in the Calvin Academy for Lifelong Learning over the past sixteen years — their enquiring minds, thoughtful questions, and ongoing interest in finding out more about the Reformation have motivated me to write this book.

Note: To help readers learn about people, places, and concepts that may be unfamiliar and to avoid breaking the flow of the text, all terms that appear in boldface are included in the glossary at the end of this book. There, readers will also find an annotated "Further Reading" section that points to various studies on the Reformation for those who are interested in further explorations of this topic.

Series Editor's Foreword

Midway along the journey of our life
I woke to find myself in some dark woods,
For I had wandered off from the straight path.

So begins the *Divine Comedy*, a classic meditation on the Christian life, written by Dante Alighieri in the fourteenth century.

Dante's three images—a journey, a dark forest, and a perplexed pilgrim—still feel familiar today, don't they?

We can readily imagine our own lives as a series of journeys, not just the big journey from birth to death, but also all the little trips from home to school, from school to job, from place to place, from old friends to new. In fact, we often feel we are simultaneously on multiple journeys that tug us in diverse and sometimes opposing directions. We recognize those dark woods from fairy tales and nightmares and the all-too-real conundrums that crowd our everyday lives. No wonder we frequently feel perplexed. We wake up shaking our heads, unsure if we know how to live wisely today or tomorrow or next week.

This series has in mind just such perplexed pilgrims. Each book invites you, the reader, to walk alongside experienced guides who will help you understand the contours of the road as well as the surrounding landscape. They will cut back the underbrush, untangle myths and misconceptions, and suggest ways to move forward.

And they will do it in books intended to be read in an evening or during a flight. Calvin Shorts are designed not just for perplexed pilgrims, but also for busy ones. We live in a complex and changing world. We need nimble ways to acquire knowledge, skills, and wisdom. These books are one way to meet those needs.

John Calvin, after whom this series is named, recognized our pilgrim condition. "We are always on the road," he said, and although this road, this life, is full of perplexities, it is also "a gift of divine kindness which is not to be refused." Calvin Shorts takes as its starting point this claim that we are called to live well in a world that is both gift and challenge.

In the *Divine Comedy*, Dante's guide is Virgil, a wise but not omniscient mentor. So too, the authors in the Calvin Shorts series don't pretend to know it all. They, like you and me, are pilgrims. And they invite us to walk with them as together we seek to live more faithfully in this world that belongs to God.

Susan M. Felch
Executive Editor
The Calvin College Press

Additional Resources

Additional online resources for *Does the Reformation Still Matter?* may be available at http://www.calvin.edu/press.

Introduction

1

In February 1548, a dozen years after **Geneva** became Protestant, some people in the city got into a major argument over salvation. The dispute took place around a sickbed at a local inn. Some Protestants had come to bring spiritual comfort to a friend who was ill. But when they arrived, they found a Catholic visitor at their friend's bedside. The visitor remarked that it would be lovely to have both the **Mass** and the preaching of the gospel at the same time. His support for a mix of key Catholic and Protestant worship practices appalled the committed Protestants in the room. To them, such a blend would be like "mixing God and Satan." Uproar ensued — hardly a restful situation for the man who was ill. The female innkeeper then got involved, telling the Protestants not to talk so much about Scripture. She added that no one is damned and that she had been born and brought up under the Mass. She finished by stating that people are as likely to be saved through Catholic as through Protestant worship.

This encounter challenges some long-held views about the Reformation. If you look at an older map of Reformation Europe, for instance, you will notice some areas labeled Catholic and others Protestant. But the Genevan vignette shows that different religious outlooks persisted even in populations that had officially chosen to accept only one branch of Christianity. Furthermore, the traditional view of the Reformation favors a top-down approach where the Reformers taught and the people listened. But here we see ordinary Genevans and visitors debating key issues of faith and making strong claims born of personal commitment. Clearly for the people at the inn that day, the Reformation mattered because life and death issues were at stake.

This theological debate around a Genevan sickbed in 1548 offers a vivid entry point into the Reformation and why it still matters today. You have picked up this book and started reading. Perhaps the title caught your eye. Perhaps you have been wondering what the Reformation was all about. Perhaps someone else felt you should read this book. Perhaps you have to learn more about the Reformation for a class, and you thought that this book at least looks mercifully short.

I should tell you at the outset that this book is not an account of the Reformation, even in condensed form. Accounts of the Reformation usually begin in the early 1500s with **Martin Luther**. But we would have to start before 1500 because pushes for major religious change began before the sixteenth century. Christianity in the west then began to break apart in the sixteenth century. Some have even adopted the plural term *Reformations* to describe the multiple paths taken by religious leaders and believers during this period. This work will mostly focus on three main branches of Protestant Christianity that emerged in the Reformation era, namely the **Lutherans**,

Anabaptists, and **Reformed**. Note that at the same time, the Catholic Church also underwent significant changes known as the Catholic Reformation. For helpful overviews of all of these topics, please go to the "Further Reading" section at the back of this book.

But overall, the topic is too large and too complex to do it justice in a few pages. Instead, this book focuses on a number of significant themes and offers reflections on why today's Christians should still care about the Reformation. Martin Luther posted his **Ninety-Five Theses** on indulgences in **Wittenberg** on October 31, 1517. This date has been widely accepted as the starting point for the Reformation in the western Christian church. But after five hundred years, does the Reformation still matter? If so, in what ways?

I am a Reformation historian deeply interested in the social history of the Reformation. I am particularly alert to its impact on **early modern** people, especially in Geneva and France. I am also a believing and practicing Christian. My roots and current practice go deep in the Reformed family of churches. By Reformed family of churches, I mean those that trace their doctrines and practices back to the Reformation in **Zurich** and Geneva. **Huldrych Zwingli** and **Heinrich Bullinger** were the main architects of the Reformation in Zurich. **John Calvin** and **Theodore Beza** were the leading Reformers in Geneva.

What I offer here are my own thoughts on the Reformation and its significance. This work makes no claim to provide definitive answers. Instead, it aims to open the way for discussion about crucial issues that emerged in the Reformation and still matter today. Here are the kinds of questions we will be considering: Is a country stronger if the majority of its people share the same beliefs? Should governments support a particular religion or worldview? If members of a particular faith feel they are under attack from their government, are these believers allowed to resist? If so, what forms can this resistance take? Can different communities of faith get along in the public arena? Can groups making competing truth claims about the fundamental values that shape their lives still find ways to coexist?

To begin, let us examine reasons why the Reformation might not matter after all. Maybe this attempt is a waste of time or even a risky proposition. Some may suggest that church history is frankly very boring and pointless. All these long-dead people with difficult names from faraway places have little relevance for today. How could the words or actions of people from so long ago have any impact on the current world? Perhaps the Reformation is simply irrelevant.

But to ignore the Reformation (or any other historical event) because it happened a long time ago is to lose awareness of a vital piece of the past that helps us understand the present. Think of it this way: people with Alzheimer's and other forms of dementia ultimately cannot make sense of the present because their memory is so badly eroded.

They forget to brush their teeth, for example, because they cannot remember what a toothbrush is for, or even how to use it. They used to know how to brush their teeth, but now they have forgotten. So the toothbrush lies unused on the counter. Their inability to make use of memory makes them unable to function in the present. In the same way, a society that ignores the past cannot come to grips with present realities shaped by that same past. For instance, the history of white dominance over other ethnic groups in the Americas since the 1500s still shapes race relations in the United States. If we disregard that history, even the best efforts to make things better today will wither away. Similarly, we cannot make sense of the present state of Christianity without turning to church history, including the Reformation.

Some modern Christians want to ignore the Reformation because of its legacy of doctrinal conflict. Debates over theology and doctrine caused much of the conflict in the Reformation. Therefore, some Christians have concluded that theology and doctrine are inherently divisive. These Christians hold that doctrinal debates should be downplayed in the wider church. Instead, Christians should find points of agreement and love their neighbors rather than fight over doctrine. In their eyes, we should forget the Reformation because it led to a major and ongoing split in the western Christian church. But if we sweep any potential areas of doctrinal conflict under the carpet, we conceal the rich legacy of faith traditions within the

Christian church. Finding common ground may seem more productive. But until we name, understand, and address these doctrinal differences, genuine unity is an ever-receding goal.

For their part, some nonreligious people see religion as one of the enduring causes of human conflict. Therefore, they may also object to any interest in the Reformation's impact in today's world. Indeed from a secular point of view, the history of religion can be seen as one long, sad tale of narrow-minded persecution and misuse of power. A nonreligious person might instead point to the more tolerant western society that has managed to free itself from this legacy of religious conflict. Thus to reflect on the long-term impact of the Reformation is simply to revisit a bad break-up. This break-up led to hostility, violence, and death. At best, a study of the Reformation's significance would provide lessons about what not to do. Yet this mindset is too one-sided. To look at the Reformation only as a source of conflict and violence is to give only a partial account of its legacy. In fact, the Reformation transformed people's theology, worship, and approach to Scripture. It made people consider whether Christians could lawfully resist their government. It also led governments and communities to consider how to deal with religious diversity. We will discuss all of these issues in the following pages.

Others, however, strongly favor learning about the Reformation. But they are less interested in the Reformation's impact on modern people. Instead, they want to score points against rival churches. Some conservative Protestants want to highlight the Reformation's significance because they are sure that Protestantism (and particularly their own branch) is right. They are equally convinced that Catholicism (or at least their take on it) is wrong. For them, knowing about the Reformation helps maintains the borders between right and wrong belief. The problem here, of course, is that these Christians only accept one assessment of the Reformation's impact: the one that agrees with them. They want to see the Reformation only as a positive force. To them, the Reformation led to the victory of true doctrine and worship over corrupt and misguided beliefs and practices. However, these strong supporters of the Reformation are also distorting its legacy.

Other Christian leaders want to focus on the Reformation to strengthen a particular branch of the Christian faith. Here the aim is to counter the growing impact of nondenominational churches. If more people become interested in the Reformation and its impact, their commitment to communities of faith rooted in the Reformation can only grow. Some church leaders also look to the Reformation to provide heroes of the faith. Martin Luther is the prime example of a Reformer who became a larger-than-life figure even in his own time. Portraits, books, and movies have made Luther famous. He was the man who stood up to the Catholic Church of his day. Yet to look to the Reformation for heroic leaders obscures the role of millions of ordinary believers whose stories are not told. Without Luther, the Reformation would never have taken off. But without men and women from all walks of life who took up the ideas of the Reformation, the movement would never have endured.

So let us not ignore the Reformation. We need to understand it to make sense of today's Christian church. Both doctrinal conflicts and religious persecution were features of the Reformation. These aspects need to be confronted rather than downplayed, even if they make us uncomfortable. At the same time, we must avoid a simplistic mining of the Reformation for heroes or for the "right answers" that will revitalize our churches.

THE REFORMATION'S CONTEXT

After setting the stage, let us turn to the topic itself. First, we need to define some terms and consider the historical context. The Reformation refers to the movement for religious change within Christianity that began in Europe in the early sixteenth century. But the Reformers were not the first to want to challenge the Catholic Church's approach. Other movements had called for substantive changes in the doctrines and practices of the church before the sixteenth century. However, none of these earlier movements managed to achieve more than a regional impact.

In England beginning in the 1350s, the **Lollards** took up many of **John Wycliffe**'s ideas. They wanted to have access to the Bible in English, not in Latin. They memorized large portions of the Scriptures in English. They criticized the church's wealth and power. But they lacked a common theological focus, and they faced persecution after a failed revolt.

In Eastern Europe beginning in the fifteenth century, the **Hussites** of **Bohemia** followed the teachings of **Jan Hus**. They too critiqued the power of the Catholic Church. They attacked what they saw as the corruption of the Catholic Church. They also wanted to receive both the bread and the wine at **Communion**. Traditionally Catholics only received the bread (Christ's body) at Communion in the form of a small round wafer placed on the tongue. The wine (Christ's blood) was more likely to be spilled during Communion as people maneuvered the cup to their lips. This **consecrated** wine was considered to be the blood of Christ; thus spilling it would be a sacrilege. So to limit the number of accidents, only the priest partook of the Communion wine. The Hussites, however, wanted to share in the full Communion of the bread and the wine, not half of it. Jan Hus was executed as a **heretic** at the **Council of Constance** in 1415, but his followers continued their pressure for reform. They successfully resisted five different crusades sent by the pope to crush the movement. By 1436, the Catholic Church agreed to let the Hussites receive both the bread and the wine at Communion. However, this practice was limited to the Hussites. The movement did not spread much beyond Bohemia.

Crucially, none of these groups had received enough political support to challenge the overall dominance of the Catholic Church. In October 1517, Luther was a little-known **monk**, priest, and professor. He did not start out with any intention of dividing Christendom or even reforming the church. So how did the Reformation take off from such small beginnings?

In 1517, no one predicted the break-up of the Catholic Church. The church was wealthy, politically influential, and well-staffed. People turned to the church at all the crucial moments of their life from birth to death. In many communities the local parish church was the heart of the community. The vast majority of those living in Western Europe at the time were Christian. Of these, pretty much everyone was Catholic. To be Catholic and to be Christian was one and the same. However, the level of devotion and commitment among Christians varied widely. Just as in today's churches, some were highly pious believers while others simply went through the motions.

Some people definitely criticized the church's wealth and the corrupt practices of some of the clergy. However, these criticisms were nothing new. Lay Christians had long complained about **simony** (the sale of positions in the church). They also objected to **pluralism** (when one cleric held several posts at the same time). Bishops were especially likely to be pluralists, and several never took up the duties of all their various offices. Here is a case in point. In 1538 at age fourteen, **Charles de Guise** became archbishop of Rheims in France. He later added the following to his resume: bishop of Metz, cardinal of Lorraine, and abbot of ten different abbeys. He did step down as bishop of Metz a year after obtaining the post. He also worked to strengthen the church in Rheims. However, there is no evidence that de Guise did more than take in the revenues of the ten abbeys he supposedly headed.

Lay people were most upset about clerical misdeeds that directly impacted them. First, some lay people resented the **absenteeism** of parish clergy caused by pluralism. Pluralist clergy could not be everywhere at once. So they tended to assign some of their many duties to less qualified colleagues. This strategy was particularly troubling because people paid for their clergy through their **tithes**. Not surprisingly parishioners did not like making do with an inferior substitute for their absent priest. Second, some lay people criticized clergy who broke their vows of chastity. Catholic clergy were supposed to be celibate. They were not supposed to have sexual relations with anyone. Congregations seemed to accept long-term relationships between a priest and a female partner. But they were quick to condemn priests who moved from partner to partner.

All told, these criticisms of the clergy's behavior were significant. But they had been voiced for a long time in the Middle Ages without leading to any fundamental changes in practice. Every so often, Catholic Church councils and leading Catholic clergy attempted to clean up these matters. But the weight of custom and the forces of inertia were too strong for any lasting reform from within to take hold at this time.

Other issues led late medieval Christians to challenge their church's practices. Again, many of these challenges had only a limited impact. One of the main intellectual trends calling for changes in the Catholic Church was **humanism**. For instance, a number of humanist scholars prior to the Reformation focused on the Bible. They studied the Bible in the original Hebrew and Greek. They prepared new translations (mostly into Latin) based on these original languages. Some also wanted the Bible to be available to ordinary people. The great humanist scholar **Erasmus** dreamed of a day when shepherds and weavers would recite the Psalms as they worked. However, these calls largely failed to reach a wider audience, often because humanists tended to write only in Latin. Meanwhile, some government leaders wanted to have more control over services traditionally provided by the church. These services included schooling and the care of the sick and the poor. Yet these power struggles between church and state rarely moved beyond the local level.

So various factors had to come together for the Reformation to take hold and have an enduring impact. The human factor was crucial. Luther and other Reformers offered a clear and effective message that went beyond criticism of corrupt practices. A movement based on criticism alone would have had no staying power. Instead,

Luther and his fellow Reformers offered a fundamental rethink about what it means to be a Christian. It turns out that doctrine and theology are crucial. The Reformers based their calls for reform on their reading and interpretation of Scripture. The message also had to reach the people. Indeed, one of Luther's biggest breakthroughs was his use of the printing press. Movable type printing had begun in Europe around 1450. The technology was still very new in Luther's day, but he made full use of it. He and others also made sure to write in the language of the people as well as in Latin, the language of the intellectual elite. Then the movement needed political protection. Luther was protected by his prince, **Frederick the Wise** of **Saxony**. Many Reformers received support and protection from city governments and rulers. Without this complex blend of factors, the Reformation could never have gotten off the ground, much less survived over the long term.

If we accept 1517 as the starting date for the Reformation, when did the Reformation end? This question is debated among historians. The problem, of course, is that assigning names and specific time frames to historical periods is a later construct. No one at the time thought, "Oh, now I'm living in the Reformation era!" or, "Oh, now we're done with the Reformation — on to the next phase!" But to keep the frame of reference of this short work manageable, we will use 1618 as our end point. In 1618, the Reformation was a century old. In that year, war broke out in Europe that lasted until 1648, a conflict known as the **Thirty Years' War**. In many ways, this war was the political working-out of conflicts that had their roots in the Reformation. The start of this war serves as a fitting bookend for this analysis.

SO WHY DID THE REFORMATION TAKE PLACE?

Many different causes led to the Reformation. A fundamental rethink about the nature of salvation, timely political protection, new technology, and committed leaders all played important roles. We need to grasp this complex network to avoid any single-facet interpretation. In the same way, when we consider the present legacy of the Reformation, we need to weigh more than one set of factors. Good historians will tell you that single-cause explanations should always be viewed with suspicion. In the next chapters, we will look at a range of reasons why the Reformation made such a difference at the time. We will also assess why the core issues raised in this era still matter today.

There is one last, important point to bear in mind to help make sense of the Reformation and its impact. The world of sixteenth-century Europe was very different from today. Early modern Christians tended to understand their faith communally rather than individually. The concept of Christendom was a very important aspect of early modern Christianity. Early modern Christians also mostly held that everyone in a given land should be of the same faith. Individual rights, religious diversity, and free choice were largely foreign concepts to early modern Christians. Understandably enough, the emergence of competing churches challenged the notion of Christendom. The solution adopted by most societies in early modern Europe was not individualism. Instead, Reformation-era governments made confessional choices for all inhabitants at the local, regional, or national level. Thus everyone in a given area was meant to adopt the same faith. Modern Christians in the west tend to object to state churches. As we shall see, some early modern Christians did too. But by and large, the state church model held sway. Bear in mind this important aspect of early modern Christianity as you read on.

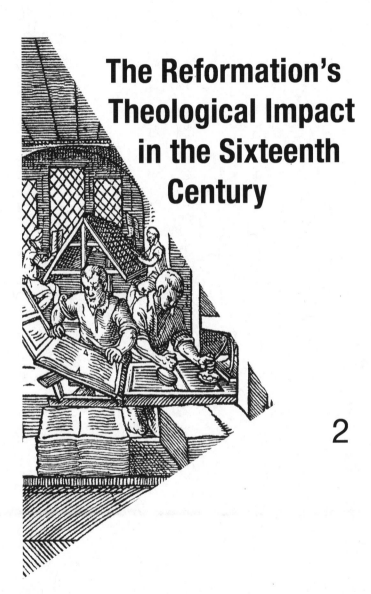

The Reformation's Theological Impact in the Sixteenth Century

2

THE REFORMATION AND THE BIBLE

The Reformers' renewed focus on the Bible shaped many of the changes in worship and belief in the period. Note that the Bible had already been available to ordinary Christians before the Reformation. Prior to 1500, both complete Bibles and many versions of parts of the Bible were produced both in Latin and in the language of the people. These pre-Reformation Bibles were available in handwritten manuscript or in early printed versions. At Mass, congregations heard readings from Scripture in Latin. Ownership of a **Book of Hours** grew more popular, especially as the printing press made these books more affordable. These prayer books contained extensive biblical extracts, mostly from the Book of Psalms. So it would not be true to claim that the Reformation brought the Bible to ordinary Christians for the first time.

Yet the Reformers placed more emphasis on Scripture than ever before. They proclaimed that the Bible was the Word of God that needed to be front and center in communal worship and private devotion. They insisted that sermons be based on a close reading and study of the Bible. The Reformers helped make the Scriptures more available in the language of the people and helped put the Bible into laypeople's hands. One of Luther's earliest undertakings was a translation of the New Testament into German, published in 1522. John Calvin's cousin, **Pierre Robert Olivétan**, produced one of the earliest complete French Bibles in print in 1535. In the same year, the first complete Bible printed in English appeared, the translation of **William Tyndale** revised and completed by **Miles Coverdale**.

This mission of Bible translation and transmission had several major consequences. First, people learned to read because they wanted to know what the Scriptures said. The Bible could also be used as a text to teach reading. Here is an example from Catholic Geneva. In the early 1530s, the early Reformer **Antoine Froment** used a covert approach to introduce Genevans to Protestant theology through the study of Scripture. He advertised classes to teach people of any age how to read and purposely used the Bible as a teaching text in these classes, thus fulfilling two goals. He ensured that people learned how to read and taught them to reflect on the practices and beliefs of their faith through reading the Bible.

The Reformers' focus on the Bible had a second major consequence. It led them to adopt different practices depending on how they read the sacred text. For example, did the Bible allow for images in churches? Were images of Christ teaching tools or a form of idolatry? What about baptism? Everyone agreed that the New Testament taught the central importance of baptism. But should babies be baptized or only people old enough to make a commitment to faith on their own?

Lutherans held that unless Scripture explicitly banned specific aspects of current worship practice, these practices were allowed. So Lutheran churches largely kept their Catholic altars, images, candles, and **vestments**. They also retained many more elements of Catholic **liturgy**. In contrast, the Swiss Reformer Huldrych Zwingli, John Calvin, and others in the Reformed branch of the church advocated a narrower reading of the Bible. For them, anything that was not specifically permitted in Scripture was therefore off-limits. So candles, vestments, images, and **frescoes** were all out. The Reformed ended up being the main proponents of **iconoclasm** (the destruction of religious images). As a result, images of all kinds were removed from churches, often violently.

For their part, the Anabaptists read the Bible even more literally. The Anabaptists were Christians who felt that Luther and Zwingli had not gone far enough on the path to Reformation. The first Anabaptists emerged in the 1520s in both the southern German and the Swiss lands. They focused above all on the New Testament. For instance, Anabaptists held that baptism should only take place after a person had come to faith. They supported adult baptism or believers' baptism as the true version of that sacrament and rejected infant baptism altogether. After all, Jesus was baptized as an adult and in Matthew 28 told his followers to make disciples, teach, and baptize. Jesus also said in Matthew 5 that no one should swear an oath — so the Anabaptists largely refused to swear oaths, whether for citizenship, for the defense of their city, or in court. In Matthew 26, Jesus said that those who live by the sword shall die by the sword. As a result, many Anabaptists adopted a pacifist stance and refused any military service. Their reading of Scripture definitely led to a highly distinctive approach to Christian living at that time.

Here is another example to show both how deep and how enduring these different readings of Scripture could be. Protestants divided into different groups because they disagreed on the meaning of Jesus' words during the Last Supper. Was the regular celebration of the **Lord's Supper** intended primarily to recall Christ's sacrifice and death ("Do this in remembrance of me")? Was Christ present in the bread and wine ("This is my body...this is my blood")? If so, was that presence physical or spiritual? Zwingli, Luther, and Calvin each read the relevant biblical passages differently and came to divergent conclusions. Zwingli and the Swiss Reformed focused on recalling what Christ did at the Last Supper. They felt that the bread and wine were there to help believers remember Christ's sacrifice. The Lutherans held that Christ was truly and physically present in the bread and the wine. They emphasized Jesus' words: "This is my body, broken for you." For their part, Calvin and his followers emphasized the spiritual presence of Christ in the sacrament. The Swiss Reformed and the Calvinists did come to agreement on their theology of the Lord's Supper. However, no compromise could be reached with the Lutherans. The divisions between the

Lutherans and the Reformed on this issue only deepened over time.

The focus on the Bible in the Reformation led to a third important outcome. It turned out that giving ordinary people access to the Bible did not always help them grasp what it meant to be Christian. This result surprised some of the Reformers. Some people living in Protestant areas simply seemed to be confused. This confusion surfaced even ten years or more after the Reformation got underway. The level of religious ignorance that Luther discovered during parish **visitations** horrified him. In the preface to his 1529 *Small Catechism*, Luther exclaimed, "Mercy! Good God! What manifold misery I beheld! The common people, especially in the villages, have no knowledge whatever of Christian doctrine…. Nevertheless, all maintain that they are Christians, have been baptized and receive the [common] holy Sacraments." These villagers claimed to be Christian. They regularly heard the Bible read and preached in church, but they could not give even a basic explanation of what they believed.

In the same vein, pastor **Charles Perrot** provided advice to his successor in his memoir about parish ministry in the Genevan countryside. Writing in the early 1560s, Perrot noted that the Epistles of Paul should be avoided in sermons. According to Perrot, their content was just too confusing for congregations. Perrot's estimate of his parishioners' ability to understand certain parts of the Bible was very low. Remember, he made this statement a full thirty years after the Reformation came to Geneva! So even though laypeople had greater access to the Bible in their own language after the Reformation, the results of this access were mixed at best.

CATECHISMS, SERMONS, AND THEOLOGY

Thus laypeople could go off-track when reading or hearing Scripture. In response, the Reformers quickly made some key changes to their strategy. Beginning in the 1520s, Protestant pastors shifted to a different way of teaching the faith. They decided that the young and ignorant in particular were to start by learning the fundamentals of their faith. This instruction came through **catechisms** rather than through Bible reading. Catechisms usually adopted a question and answer format. This training required participants to memorize answers on various aspects of faith and practice. Protestant catechisms focused on core beliefs as articulated in the Lord's Prayer, the Ten Commandments, and the **Apostles' Creed**. These catechism manuals became a key aspect of every church's toolkit. Furthermore, everyone was to attend church regularly to hear sermons. Pastors' sermons focused on explaining God's Word and its meaning and implications to the people. Pastors, therefore, had to deepen their knowledge of Scripture through preparation for catechism sessions and sermons.

This reading and reflection on Scripture led church leaders to recast their understanding of key theological issues. These topics included the nature of human sin and the role of God and of human beings in salvation. Traditional Catholic doctrine had taught that all humans are tainted by original sin. This sin was washed away by baptism, which included the ritual of **exorcism**. Human beings still sinned after baptism, but they could confess to a priest, repent, and be forgiven through the sacrament of **penance**. The Reformers' significant insight on this topic was to assert that even after baptism, sin was a singular word. Sin was a state of being, not a series of wrong thoughts, words, or deeds.

This perspective signaled both a greater burden and a greater deliverance. Human beings could do nothing to save themselves from their sin. Repeated confession of even the smallest sins, as Luther discovered, did not provide any enduring assurance of being right with God. During his years as an **Augustinian friar**, Luther worried constantly about sins he had committed. He confessed these minor sins over and over again, but found no relief. His study of Paul's Letter to the Romans as he prepared his lectures at Wittenberg University changed Luther's outlook. Romans 1:17 reads, "The just shall live by faith." This statement helped Luther realize that he could never deserve God's forgiveness by his own efforts. Salvation came through grace alone and faith alone, not through one's works. Only through Christ's sacrificial death on the cross could God's unmerited grace lift the weight of sin from human souls.

The Reformers' emphasis on God's grace as the sole agent of salvation freed the spiritually anxious from endless stress. They could stop worrying over what they needed to do to be justified in the sight of God. However, this teaching also opened the door to other questions. For one thing, salvation by grace alone left God's intent unclear: was everyone saved? If not, and if people were not saved at least in part on the basis of their deeds, what were the criteria? It is important to note that **predestination**, the doctrine that God in his unsearchable wisdom had chosen some for salvation and condemned others, did not originate in the Reformation era. Instead, it found its scriptural basis in Paul's Letter to the Romans. **Augustine of Hippo** and **Thomas Aquinas** also developed this doctrine in their writings. In the sixteenth century, Luther, Calvin, and others highlighted this doctrine. For Calvin, predestination was a comfort especially for religious exiles and those persecuted for their faith. In spite of their trials and their significant losses, they could rest assured in the knowledge that God had not abandoned them. Nothing that happened to them could make them fall from God's hand.

Not surprisingly, the doctrine of predestination also proved divisive. Some felt predestination made people into puppets and turned God into an arbitrary judge. Others were tempted to anticipate God's judgment. These Christians wanted to decide for themselves who was among **the elect** and who was among **the reprobate**.

Furthermore, the comfort that the doctrine of predestination was meant to provide could prove elusive. Some Christians, whether Catholic or Protestant, searched anxiously for signs of divine election in their life. Some Catholics worried whether they were doing enough to contribute to their salvation. After the Reformation, some Reformed Protestants were equally plagued by fears. Were they in fact among the elect? In effect, for some Christians the situation had come full circle. Neither a focus on their own deeds (good or bad) nor a reliance on God's election could bring assurance of salvation to their troubled hearts.

Overall, the Reformation's impact on theology was wide-ranging. Reformers used Scripture to reflect on the core issues of human sin and salvation. Their insights on key topics often diverged. But they were willing to move beyond a critique of the Catholic Church's practices and turn instead to major theological issues. This vital theological project highlights the Reformation's importance. However, lay Christians may well have missed the nuances of these doctrinal debates. What congregations were more likely to notice were the very visible changes in worship that stemmed from these theological insights.

The Reformation's Impact on Worship and the Laity in the Sixteenth Century

3

In many cases, the transformation in worship that took place during the Reformation was dramatic. Some Protestant churches retained many aspects of Catholic ritual. Others, however, reframed their entire pattern of worship based on their reading of the Bible and their understanding of early church practices. Catholics had seven sacraments. Protestants limited that number to two: baptism and the Lord's Supper, because these were the only two sacraments Jesus had taught. Catholics worshipped in Latin. Protestants worshipped in their mother tongue. Catholic worship focused on the altar and the sacrament of the Mass. Protestant worship focused mainly on the pulpit and the sermon. The content of the sermon was very important. In Calvin's Geneva, for instance, people were to listen attentively to the hour-long sermon and remember what it was about.

LUTHERAN WORSHIP

A person who walked into a Lutheran church in 1550 might have found it difficult at first glance to decide whether the church was Lutheran or Catholic. Lutheran church interiors still looked like Catholic churches, with ornate altars and widespread use of religious images. Luther was willing to continue many aspects of Catholic worship. His approach was psychologically astute. In the first years of the Reformation in particular, he argued against those who wanted to quicken the pace of change in worship. He noted that making such changes too quickly might cause weaker brethren to stumble. In Luther's mind, the "rightness" of the changes did not outweigh the danger of losing those who remained attached to their traditional worship practices. Although the language of Lutheran worship services largely moved from Latin to the **vernacular**, Lutheran liturgies still retained the structure of the Latin Mass. However, there were some significant changes. Lutherans received both the wine and the bread at Communion, and sermons became a central part of the regular Sunday worship.

REFORMED WORSHIP

In Reformed areas, careful reading of Scripture led Reformers and lay people to look at their church buildings and worship practices with new eyes. Reformed Protestants in Zurich, Geneva, France, the Netherlands, and Scotland largely made a clean sweep of Catholic worship. Anyone entering Saint Pierre Cathedral in Geneva in 1520 and again thirty years later in 1550 could not miss the differences. In 1520, Geneva's cathedral had a high altar. The cathedral also featured many small side chapels, each with its own altar, where Masses could be celebrated. By some estimates, as many as two hundred Masses a week took place in Catholic Geneva. Many of these were memorial Masses, paid for by money from the deceased person's estate or from relatives. The priest celebrated Mass in Latin, facing the altar, and therefore with his back to the congregation. Meanwhile, the faithful recited their own prayers in an undertone. The cathedral was full of images of saints, of the Virgin Mary, and of Christ.

Once Geneva's voting population officially voted to accept Reformed Protestantism as the city's official faith in 1536, the whole pattern of their worship changed. Images, statues, candles, and vestments were gone. More than that, the focus of communal worship shifted. Whereas their Catholic worship had been oriented around the altar where the Mass was celebrated, now their attention moved to the pulpit. Catholics in Geneva stood or knelt during worship. After the Reformation, Genevans largely sat in church, especially during the hour-long sermon. Therefore benches had to be installed, and these benches were oriented around the pulpit. In fact, when Reformed Protestants could build their own churches rather than repurpose Catholic churches, they made several key changes. Catholic churches were usually cross-shaped, with the high altar as the focal point at the end of the **nave**. Newly built Protestant churches (in Scotland and in France, for instance) tended to be built in the round. In these buildings, the pulpit stood in the center.

In Geneva, church-goers were to listen attentively to the sermon and remember the core message. Indeed at their weekly meetings on Thursdays, the Genevan **consistory** regularly asked those appearing before them to recall the past Sunday's sermon. Reformed pastors in Geneva, as in other Protestant areas, also largely eliminated popular worship-related practices. These included the use of holy water, prayers to the saints or the Virgin Mary, pilgrimages, making the sign of the cross, and prayers for the dead. All of these practices were deemed superstitious and banned.

ANABAPTIST WORSHIP

The first Anabaptists were early and eager adopters of the Reformation. They emerged among Lutheran and Reformed believers, but felt these Christians had not gone far enough in being faithful to Scripture. The Anabaptists rejected vestments, images, and anything that might distract believers from the worship of God. So their approach to worship was starkly different than traditional Catholic practice. Because they were heavily persecuted in Western Europe in the sixteenth century, they rarely built churches. Anabaptists also tended to be suspicious of any push to set a given space aside as holy. Instead, they worshipped in barns or in private homes or outdoors.

Again because of persecution, records of Anabaptist worship practices are sparse. Evidence that does survive shows that their worship included prayers, singing, Bible readings, and exhortation. Indeed, their sermons focused mainly on exhorting the congregation to continue in their faith walk. Some Anabaptist communities encouraged members of the congregation to share their insights with the rest of the group during worship. Overall, they stressed the communal aspect of worship. Therefore they resisted any push to recreate a hierarchy of roles in the church.

RESPONSES TO CHANGES IN WORSHIP

All told, these worship changes were dramatic. Not surprisingly, some people found the new ways of worship hard to accept. In Geneva, some who attended these new services fell asleep in the middle of the sermon. Others tried to sneak out early. One Catholic eyewitness reported that worship in Reformed Geneva was like being in a school. That was not a compliment. Some who objected to these changes in worship may well have wanted to continue being Catholic. For instance when the government of **Edward VI** ordered everyone to use the Protestant **Book of Common Prayer**, protests erupted in strongly Catholic parts of England. One southern English uprising in 1549 is even known as the **Prayer Book Rebellion**.

In other cases, however, it seems that even supporters of the key theological teachings of Protestantism were simply bewildered by the transformation of their lifelong worship practices. The people of Cornwall in the southwest of England objected to the Book of Common Prayer. They were especially unhappy about worshipping in English and called for a return to the Latin Mass. Their mother tongue was Cornish, not English, so Latin seemed by far more familiar and comfortable to them.

MUSIC IN CHURCH

One element of Protestant worship that did prove popular over time, however, was congregational singing. Not all Protestant churches took up this practice. In Zurich, for instance, Zwingli felt that any music in church was a distraction. Calvin, however, adopted the practice of Psalm singing that he heard in Strasbourg. He motivated a team of poets and composers to work on versifying the Psalms and setting them to music. By 1562, the first complete **metrical (versified) Psalter** in French came off the presses. This **Genevan Psalter** was quickly translated into other languages. The practice of singing metrical Psalms, often using the melodies from the Genevan Psalter, spread across Europe. Reformed Christians in the Netherlands, Hungary, Scotland, and eventually Puritan New England sang these Psalms in unison in church and in harmony at home.

Music also played a key role among the Lutherans and the Anabaptists. Luther and his fellow pastors wanted to encourage more congregational singing, so they developed the use of hymns and chorales. Anabaptists also sang hymns. Many of these were composed by believers in captivity or condemned to death for their Anabaptist views. These martyrs' songs formed the core of Anabaptist singing.

All told, these major changes in worship practices highlight the Reformation's significant impact among ordinary believers. These rituals did take hold. They shaped the identity of faith communities in remarkable ways. For instance, officially the **Holy Roman Empire**'s policy from 1555 onwards was that the people of a given area should adopt their ruler's faith. Yet when **John Sigismund**, Duke of Brandenburg, became Reformed in 1613, his people largely remained Lutheran, as they had been since 1539. Sources recount difficult encounters between the Reformed clergy appointed by the duke and the Lutheran parishioners who needed their services. At one point, a Lutheran butcher asked his Reformed pastor to conduct a baptism. The butcher wanted to have a Lutheran baptism for his baby son. Lutheran baptisms featured **anointing** and exorcism. These practices were not part of a Reformed baptism. To ensure the pastor's compliance with Lutheran practices, the butcher came to the baptism armed with his cleaver. For this butcher, only a Lutheran baptism was a real baptism. **Brandenburg** had only been Lutheran for seventy-five years. Yet that was long enough for lay people to cherish these specific worship practices.

THE ROLE OF LAY PEOPLE

The story of the Lutheran butcher with his cleaver and the earlier account of the bedside debate over salvation in Geneva help us hear lay people's voices in the Reformation era. They show how involved lay people were in matters of faith. As the Reformation took hold, the role of lay people in the church also changed significantly. Among Catholics, leadership had largely remained in the hands of the clergy. Lay Catholics could exert financial influence in the church if they were wealthy. If they were rulers, they could exert political pressure on the church. Parents, especially mothers, played a key role in teaching their children the prayers, basic beliefs, and practices of Catholicism. But otherwise, the voice of lay Catholics in the church, particularly in leadership, was rather muted.

In contrast, the Reformation gave lay people a greater role in the church in a number of ways. For theological and practical reasons, Luther reinforced the idea of salvation by grace alone, not tied to a Christian's status or occupation. Baptism made all Christians spiritually equal. Clergy were not somehow more holy or closer to God. They were not in a separate spiritual category.

Luther's message of spiritual equality struck a chord with many lay people in the German lands. Some even took the message in directions Luther had not anticipated. In the 1520s, for instance, some peasants called for the right to select their own pastors. Others refused to pay the traditional tithe to the church. The **Peasants' War** of 1525 proved to be a watershed. Inspired at least in part by Luther's ideas, peasants in the German lands made a series of economic and social demands. They supported their claims with scriptural references in the **Twelve**

Articles of the Peasants. The German nobility crushed the uprising. By the later 1520s, Luther backed away from his earlier support for pious lay people's ability to interpret the meaning of Scripture. In a visible sign of the changing outlook, the figure of the pious peasant that had been a stock character in early Lutheran dialogues largely disappeared by 1530.

Yet lay voices continued to strengthen in the Reformation era. Due to persecution, the **radical** wing of the Reformation developed in a decentralized way. For example, among early Anabaptists, spiritual leadership remained largely in lay hands. In some instances lay people, both women and men, offered prophecies. Anabaptists had no seminaries or training centers. Instead, they chose their pastors from among the members of the congregation. Thus lay people grew in importance by selecting church leaders at the congregational level.

The Anabaptists insisted on adult or believers' baptism before someone could join them. Those who took this step and were baptized had to make the choice to do so for themselves. No parent or godparent could make promises on their behalf, as was the case for infant baptism. Anabaptists also knew the risks they faced of attack by other Christians. The practice of adult baptism and the likelihood of persecution meant that Anabaptists were more apt to have reflected deeply about their faith before joining. Hence their level of active participation in what was a voluntary community was strikingly high.

For their part, the Reformed took a different approach to the issue of lay people's role in the church. They channeled lay commitment into the offices of **elder** and **deacon**. Calvin laid out the need for women to serve as **deaconesses** to help women who were poor or ill. However, his suggestion gained little traction. As a result, the offices of elder and deacon remained in the hands of men. Elders were to assist the pastor in the works of spiritual care and discipline of the community. Meanwhile, deacons were tasked with a range of responsibilities. They managed the church's resources, served as liturgical assistants, and oversaw poor relief.

In some areas, the Reformed church was a minority in a larger Catholic community, as in France and the southern Netherlands. In these churches, elders and deacons played a crucial role. These lay leaders helped ensure the survival of these threatened communities. Even if its pastor was captured or forced out by the Catholic authorities, a Reformed congregation could continue to function under the leadership of its elders and deacons. In France, particularly in the 1550s and early 1560s, the Reformed faith spread rapidly and outpaced the availability of pastors. In this situation, congregations under lay leadership emerged and were recognized as valid churches. These communities could gather and have Bible readings, Psalm singing, prayers, and even some preaching. Without a pastor, they could not celebrate baptisms and the Lord's Supper. They also could not establish a consistory. In all other respects, however, a church led by elders and deacons could operate successfully.

Thus the changes in worship and lay roles in the church during the Reformation era were both dramatic and far-reaching. At the same time, the role of the clergy underwent significant transformations. Above all, the clergy's role changed in relation to the growing power of the state.

The Reformation's Impact on Church and State Relations

4

THE ROLE OF THE CLERGY

The role of lay people grew in Protestant churches during the Reformation. At the same time, the status of the clergy altered as well. The most noticeable change when a community went from Catholic to Protestant was the drop in the number of clergy. In most instances, religious orders were dissolved or departed for Catholic territories. For example, the **nuns** of the convent of Poor Clares in Geneva faced strong pressure to adopt Protestantism. In the 1530s, the newly Protestant government ordered them to leave their nunnery and return to secular life. Like nuns elsewhere, when compelled to listen to Protestant preaching, the Genevan nuns put wool in their ears. Although one nun did leave the convent to return to her family, the others held firm. By 1535, the Poor Clares departed from Geneva and headed to the nearby Catholic territory of Savoy. There they rebuilt their community.

The disappearance of monks and nuns, **friars**, and **chantry priests** visibly altered the balance between clergy and lay people. In some early modern cities before the Reformation, priests and men and women in religious orders formed up to ten percent of the population. In a city of five thousand people, as many as five hundred could be priests, friars, monks, or nuns. After the Reformation, the same community might only have ten to twenty pastors in total. That dramatic shift would not go unnoticed. It is true that in some Lutheran areas, nunneries continued to operate. These convents offered an option for women outside of marriage and family life. However, across the board in Protestant areas the number of clergy plummeted. Alongside the decrease in the size of the clerical corps was a change in their private life. The Reformers advocated marriage and fatherhood for pastors because they found no biblical warrant for priestly celibacy. Thus the model of the celibate priest, monk, or friar was cast aside. In its place emerged the image of the pastor as exemplary husband and father.

The Reformation also brought changes to the clergy's civil status. Prior to the Reformation, the clergy were a separate category of people, governed by their own laws. Ultimately they were answerable to the hierarchy of the church, all the way up to the pope. This situation continued to hold true in Catholic areas throughout the early modern era. In territories that adopted Protestantism, however, the clergy lost that independence. These pastors no longer held a separate legal status. Instead, they were answerable to the civil authorities. In fact, the civil authorities paid the pastors' salaries from the income that lay people provided through the tithe. This tithe was now paid not to the church but to the government. In essence, these pastors became civil servants. In many instances they had to swear oaths of loyalty and obedience to the political leaders.

STATE CONTROL OF CHURCHES

Indeed, state control over the church in Protestant areas grew stronger in the Reformation era. This expansion reshaped the balance of power between church and state. The Lutheran and Reformed churches that relied on civil authorities for protection were particularly affected. Luther appealed to the princes and magistrates of the German lands to support the Reformation. He did so because it seemed that the movement was under threat from the powerful Catholic Church. Many of the city councils and princes responded positively to his appeal. Some may well have been motivated by Luther's religious message.

At the same time, government officials could see clear practical advantages to protecting the nascent Protestant church. Once the Reformation got underway, they took over Catholic Church lands that could be appropriated by the state and sold for a handsome profit. For instance in England prior to the Reformation, the Catholic Church owned anywhere from a quarter to a third of the territory in the country. Most of this land was in the hands of the monasteries, abbeys, and nunneries. Already in the 1520s, early in King **Henry VIII**'s reign, some of these communities were shut down. Their assets were then transferred to fund other causes. These included financing Oxford and Cambridge colleges. The pace of dissolution of these monasteries, abbeys, and nunneries accelerated in the mid-1530s. As a result, the king dramatically boosted his income. Wealthy landowners bought many of these properties from the crown to extend their own lands.

Political leaders were thus quick to acquire church lands in Protestant areas. However, they also expanded their influence over the church in other ways. For example, secular rulers now oversaw education and the care of the poor. Many of the costs of these services were met by income taken over from the Catholic Church. As already noted, tithes were still collected but were paid into the government's coffers. In England, Scotland, and Wales after the Reformation, the right to appoint a pastor to a particular church often transferred from the local bishop or monastery to a local landowner. The landowner could then pay the pastor less than the amount collected from the tithes provided by the parishioners, and the landowner would happily pocket the difference.

These examples and others show how governments could see real practical advantages in supporting the Protestant churches. At the same time, they also seemed to value their new role as arbitrators in religious debates. In the early years of the Reformation in particular, Reformers called on their government officials to hold open debates. The concept of debates over theological issues was not new. The new features were the use of the vernacular and the presence of the magistrates not as witnesses to the debates but as judges. Government officials were to weigh the arguments on both sides and decide whether their area should remain Catholic or adopt Protestantism.

Two such debates were held in the Swiss city of Zurich in January and October of 1523. The Zurich city council served as arbitrator and decision-maker. These debates were held in public and in the language of the people. The gatherings supposedly allowed both Catholic and Reformed leaders to make their case. In fact, the results of the debates were pretty much a foregone conclusion. As a result of the disputations of 1523, the Zurich magistrates ordered clergy to preach only from Scripture. The city council ultimately banned the Mass and images in Zurich's churches. Similar debates took place in other Swiss cities in the 1520s and 1530s.

In many ways, the Reformers were smart to call on government leaders for a verdict on which religious teachings to adopt. The early Reformation needed the protection of princes and city governments. Without it, the early Reformers would not have had the freedom to proclaim their teachings and gain popular support. The state church model also ensured that the population of a given area all followed the same beliefs and practices of the faith. Government-issued mandates in Geneva, for instance, gave instructions to the population. Genevans were to attend church, bring their babies for baptism, and avoid an extensive list of banned Catholic practices and rituals. Reformers could also make use of state authority to deal with religious opponents. These objectors could face banishment, jail time, or even execution. Across the board, therefore, both the Lutheran and the Reformed churches gained a great deal from having the government on their side. Yet this protection came at a cost.

The Reformers asked for and received government support. But secular leaders did not simply want to help the Protestant church in its time of need. Instead, they aimed to continue to have a say in the running of the church. The Reformers may have imagined that the government's aid was only a temporary measure. However, the princes and magistrates saw matters very differently. For their part, government leaders felt that the community's money funded the church and paid the pastors. Therefore, it was only right that these pastors should be answerable to those who were paying them.

Governments also took their religious mission seriously. Their duty was to shape the beliefs of their community and ensure doctrinal orthodoxy. For instance in England, the state church model was particularly strong after Henry VIII broke with Rome. The English Parliament ended up taking on the duties of a church assembly. In 1539, for example, Parliament ratified Henry VIII's **Act of Six Articles**. This act laid out the core doctrinal beliefs all English people were to hold. Some rulers also felt that it was dangerous to give the church too much leeway. These political leaders wanted to avoid going back to a church-dominated society. Thus in the Swiss Reformed cities, the magistrates firmly kept the power of church discipline in their own hands. For example they refused to allow church leaders the power to bar or admit people to the Lord's Supper.

THE ANABAPTIST CRITIQUE

The government's active role in the affairs of these churches opened the door for Anabaptist critiques. Anabaptists charged that the mainline Lutheran and Reformed leaders had strayed from the model of the New Testament church. In the New Testament, people made a conscious choice to join the Christians. Governments played no role in the oversight of churches. Similarly, the Anabaptists had created faith communities without state involvement. Their pastors were not paid by the state. No early modern government in Western Europe adopted Anabaptism as their state church. Instead, Anabaptist communities regulated their own affairs and handled disputes or disaffection internally. Their system of church discipline was highly effective. It was rooted in the community's acceptance of norms of behavior and belief. Those who stepped outside these boundaries and refused to repent could face the **ban**. The community was to shun or ostracize the recalcitrant member until he or she showed signs of genuine repentance. So for the Anabaptists, the regulation of church life was an entirely internal affair. From their point of view, the government had no role to play in church life. The church and the government were entirely separate realms.

In response to the Anabaptist critique, John Calvin pointed to a different biblical model. Calvin compared the state church of his day to the kingdom of Israel in the

Old Testament. In his sermons, he regularly compared the people of Geneva to the people of Israel. The pastors of the city were like the Old Testament prophets. The magistrates were like Israel's kings. These parallels could both justify the role of the state in the Reformed church and encourage governments to make decisions that would help the church thrive.

But what if the government and the state church were in conflict? This problem was especially acute in the **Dutch Republic**. In 1581, this area of seven provinces had broken away from Spanish Catholic control. In doing so, the seven northern provinces split off from ten southern provinces. In the north, the state church was officially Reformed. However right up to the late 1500s, the Reformed were a minority in the Dutch Republic. In fact, the population was a mix of Lutherans, Catholics, Reformed, and Anabaptists. No one group held a numerical majority.

Reformed church leaders in the Dutch Republic were constantly frustrated. They were the state church. However, the government left room for other communities of faith. In particular, pastors resented having to marry and baptize all comers. The government insisted that these services be provided to anyone, regardless of their church membership status. The Reformed pastors also wanted to enforce stricter observance of the faith. However, government officials were more moderate. Pastors objected to the reluctance of magistrates to ban activities that competed with Sunday worship. These activities included going to taverns or target practice. Yet government leaders continued to resist Reformed pressure to have everyone conform to Reformed norms of behavior and religious practice. They also held strongly to their right to appoint teachers and ratify the nomination of pastors and elders. Government leaders wanted to assert their oversight of the Reformed church. They also wanted to select candidates who mirrored their moderate stance. Meanwhile, the pastors feared that the civil authorities would select more doctrinally flexible candidates. Church leaders saw these government actions as unwarranted interference.

Overall, the Reformation reconfigured the beliefs and practices of Christians in early modern Europe. The Reformers' focus on Scripture and its teachings reframed beliefs and reshaped worship. The movement also gave laypeople more of a voice in leadership. Furthermore, the Reformation altered the status of the clergy. State support ended up giving rulers more control over the church. So the Reformation mattered at the time because it offered new ways of thinking about God, faith, and the Christian life. Early modern Christians of various stripes disagreed fervently about many of these matters. However, different groups got enough breathing room to practice their version of Christianity without being persecuted out of existence. Thus the Reformation opened the door to multiple approaches to these issues of faith and Christian life.

Turning to the present, what significance does the Reformation still hold for today? Are there aspects of the Reformation that still resonate in our world? The next chapter will consider reasons why the Reformation still matters after five hundred years.

The Reformation
Still Matters
Today

5

It is very tempting to credit the Reformation with many of the positive aspects of the modern western world-view. For instance, some claim that the Reformation led to the growth of religious toleration. Others argue that the Reformation fostered the modern spirit of critical enquiry. **Max Weber** famously linked Calvinism and capitalism. Yet others credit the Reformation for the rise of the nation-state. In fact to its supporters, the Reformation laid the groundwork for much of modern western culture. However, it is almost impossible to connect the Reformation's stance on these issues and current realities. Too much time has elapsed. Too many other movements have influenced societies in the meantime. These include the **Enlightenment** and the **scientific revolution**. Most historians credit these currents, rather than the Reformation, for the main features of the modern western mindset.

THE CENTRALITY OF SCRIPTURE

Yet some features of the Reformation continue to engage hearts and minds today. One key aspect is the ongoing focus on the Bible. One of the Reformers' great gifts to Christianity has been their call to put Scripture at the center of the life of faith. Some of this emphasis was born of doctrinal conflict. The Reformers concurred that the

Word of God in Scripture, not church tradition, held authority for believers. But what if theologians disagreed about what the Bible said? The Reformers had to come to terms with competing doctrines rooted in Scripture. They therefore spent significant time and energy interpreting the Bible. For example, the Reformer **Balthasar Hubmaier** was one of the most effective Anabaptist theologians. He carefully compared adult and infant baptism in the light of Scripture. He pointed out that the Reformed defense of infant baptism rested on a weak analogy. He noted that the Reformed saw infant baptism as the heir of the Old Testament rite of circumcision. He reminded the supporters of infant baptism that Jesus never commended this practice in the Gospels. Hubmaier provided a well-grounded defense of the Anabaptist practice of believers' baptism. His approach forced Zwingli in turn to deepen his analysis of Scripture to buttress the Reformed position.

More generally, early modern pastors and lay people alike put the Bible at the center of their life of faith. Future pastors dove into the Old and New Testaments during their seminary studies. Protestant seminaries in Reformation Europe regularly offered courses in Hebrew. Greek was already taught at the high school level. These courses enabled a more thorough study of the biblical text. By the early 1600s, the Dutch Reformed University of Leiden was the European leader in the study of ancient languages. Lay people too became increasingly grounded in Scripture. From the later 1500s onward, lists of goods in wills from

Protestant homes regularly included the Bible. In many instances, the Bible was one of the few books a family might own.

Thus the ongoing focus on Scripture is part of the Reformation's enduring legacy for today's church. People around the world can access the Bible in print or in various digital formats. Wycliffe Bible Translators and other groups have been working to get the Bible to everyone in their mother tongue. People may still disagree about what the Bible means. But almost everyone can now read or hear God's Word in their own language. The Reformers gave a tremendous impetus to making the Bible available to everyone. Currently, small group Bible studies are a hallmark of nearly every Christian denomination around the world. Within their own church or ecumenically, Christians are still hearing, reading, and sharing Scripture.

RETHINKING THE RELATIONSHIP BETWEEN POLITICAL LEADERS AND THEIR PEOPLE

The Reformers' emphasis on the centrality of Scripture in doctrine and worship still persists today. But other issues emerged in the break-up of western Christendom that continue to shape Christianity in our day. For instance, Christians still debate the right of resistance. In other words, is it ever acceptable for a believer to resist the actions of a legitimate government? What forms might this resistance take? In chapter thirteen of his Letter to the Romans, the apostle Paul taught that Christians must obey their governing authorities. The same instruction can also be found in 1 Peter 2.

But how far should this obedience go? In the Reformation era, this question became vital. Protestants in majority Catholic areas asked what they should do when pursued as heretics by their own government. In France, for instance, the French Catholic government arrested, tried, and executed French Protestants for heresy. John Calvin responded to this very difficult situation. He stated that princes, nobles, and lower-level government officials (the "lesser magistrates") had the right to oppose the actions of a persecuting monarch or central government. However, he also said that individual believers who were private citizens had no right to resist their rulers. At most, these ordinary citizens could offer passive resistance when their faith was under attack. As the French religious wars dragged on, calls for active resistance became stronger. The deaths of thousands of French Protestants at the hands of Catholics during the **Saint Bartholomew's Day Massacre** in 1572 were a turning point. Later Reformed writers championed the right of resistance. These writers argued that the monarch had broken the covenant that bound him to God and to his people. The king had failed in his duty to protect his people and had even used force against them. Therefore his people were released from their duty of obedience.

The Scottish and English Reformers **John Knox** and

Christopher Goodman also advocated resistance in the mid-sixteenth century. They wanted to mobilize Protestants in Scotland and England against their Catholic rulers. Both men had personal reasons for supporting resistance. Knox's friend and mentor **George Wishart** was burned alive for heresy in the Scottish university town of **Saint Andrews** in 1546. Knox then joined in the forcible occupation of Saint Andrews' Castle. The occupiers eventually had to surrender to Catholic forces and were sentenced (Knox among them) to row on French galleys. For his part, Goodman lost his employment at Oxford University when the Catholic queen **Mary I** came to the throne. He ended up going into exile from England in 1554. Knox and Goodman went considerably further in their arguments for resistance than Calvin had. The two men wrote that even ordinary lay believers had not just a right but a duty to resist any ruler who threatened the practice of the Reformed faith. Goodman went so far as to advocate killing such a ruler.

These Protestant thinkers were among the first to address key questions of political theory. Many of them saw the dangers of anarchy that could result from Christians matching force with force. Yet as time went on, pressure on religious minorities mounted. In response, the rhetoric of resistance grew more heated. Some Catholics also began to follow the Protestants' lead. Hardline Catholics began to favor active resistance both in theory and in practice. Indeed, radical Catholics killed a number of Protestant political leaders in the later 1500s and early 1600s. For instance the hardline Catholic Balthasar Gérard shot the Dutch ruler **William of Orange** in 1584. The French kings **Henri III** and **Henri IV** were also killed by ultra-Catholics. A **Dominican** lay brother, Jacques Clément, stabbed Henri III to death in 1589. In 1610, a Catholic visionary named François Ravaillac used the same method to kill Henri IV.

Early modern resistance theories still resonate today. These ideas resurfaced in the English Civil War in the 1600s and in the American war of independence in the later 1700s. In today's world, most people living in democracies rightly refuse to use force to change their government. Regular democratic elections, term limits, and checks and balances are the main ways to prevent tyranny. But the call of John Calvin and other Reformers to non-violent resistance by ordinary citizens has endured. Committed Christians' protection of their Jewish neighbors in Nazi Germany provides one example. The church-led civil rights campaign in the United States in the 1950s and 1960s provides another.

Reformation-era thinkers also debated what it means to govern. What are the duties of governments towards their people? Are citizens meant to honor their government? If so, in what ways? In the 1700s, several writers pursued these questions on the rights and duties of people and their government leaders. One of these was **Jean-Jacques Rousseau**, who was born and raised as a Genevan

Protestant. One of his most famous works was *The Social Contract* (1762). Rousseau's analysis of the rights and duties of governments and citizens built on the Reformation's covenantal emphasis. The idea that political leaders and the wider population have mutual obligations to each other is helpful. Governments' mandate to remember their core duty to care for their people guards against power-grabbing. Currently some politicians seem to have lost sight of this duty in their quest for power. The call for populations to respect their political leaders also runs counter to current trends. Cynicism, suspicion, and knee-jerk hostility seem instead to be the order of the day. Our contemporary political discourse is often toxic. The Reformation's focus on a mutual covenant between government and people would help reset the conversation. Early modern Christians had to think through how to proceed when political power and religious choices were at odds. Worldwide, today's citizens and political leaders can benefit greatly from these insights.

COMPETING BELIEF SYSTEMS

A third key issue arose in the Reformation era and continues to generate significant discussion. How should one respond to competing belief systems within a given society? Today, the ideals of religious diversity and toleration are central to western culture. Yet these principles have weakened in the face of perceived threats. In the last decades, for instance, most of the fear and reluctance to make room for others' beliefs has centered on non-Muslims' view of Islam. Radical Muslims have committed acts of terrorism. At the same time, many in the west feel that Islam is not tolerant of other beliefs. Therefore, some societies and individuals have opposed the free practice of Islam on an equal footing with other faiths. More generally, thoughtful individuals wonder about toleration. Should all beliefs and faiths be accepted? Is there one truth and many false beliefs, or many versions of the one truth? Or is there no one truth but only human approximations? How (if at all) can one balance holding to a specific faith as true while at the same time making room for those who hold other beliefs? Do the choices boil down to making a strong truth claim and condemning all other beliefs, or ending up with relativism where any and all belief systems are equally valid and equally accepted? Are there any other options?

These same questions emerged in the Reformation era. As western Christendom fractured and divided, pastors and lay people alike had to confront these issues. It is important to admit that the Reformation era was not a tolerant age. The power of the state was used to compel belief. Governments dealt harshly with those who did not accept the official beliefs. This reality was true across the board. Protestants were no more tolerant than Catholics. Every faith group that managed to acquire state support of some kind targeted public expressions of other beliefs.

For example when Henry VIII broke with the papacy,

he did not usher in a more tolerant age. He did not want his people to look to Rome, but he also rejected Protestant doctrine. During his reign, both Catholic supporters of papal supremacy and those who adopted Protestant theology and refused to recant were executed. In the reign of his Catholic daughter, Mary I, around three hundred English Protestants were executed for their faith. Under her Protestant half-sister, **Elizabeth I**, around two hundred Catholics were executed. Most of these were Jesuit priests. Thus, toleration in the modern sense found no foothold in early modern England.

Official documents from the time also left little room for religious compromise, though sometimes governments did provide for toleration in official edicts. One example is the **Edict of Nantes** in France in 1598. This royal edict provided toleration for French Protestant **Huguenots** but strictly limited their rights because overall the aim was to have Huguenots return to the official Catholic faith of France. Thus the Edict of Nantes and others used a narrow definition of toleration, based on the Latin verb *tolerare*. Toleration in this sense meant to bear with something, usually only for a limited time. As a result, political legislation in the Reformation did not directly lead to a more tolerant society.

Yet when no single faith held the majority, some governments put in place systems that allowed for religious coexistence. The prime example in early modern Western Europe is the Dutch Republic. The state church was the

Reformed faith. But the Dutch government allowed those who were not Reformed to practice their faith in private. So Lutherans, Anabaptists, Catholics, Jews, and others found ways to practice their faith undercover. These religious minorities took the opportunity to stretch the definition of "private." In Amsterdam in the late seventeenth century, for instance, Catholics bought up rows of private homes. The Catholics then removed the interior walls and created a place of worship for their community. From the outside, the row still looked like a set of private homes. But inside a quasi-public place of Catholic worship had been created.

For their part, theologians responded to religious pluralism in early modern Europe in a range of ways. Some issued blanket rejections of others' beliefs. In their polemical writings in particular, the Reformers took a hardline stance on doctrine. They condemned other Christians for holding to wrong beliefs. For instance, Reformers regularly referred to the pope as the Antichrist. They also attacked the Mass as idolatry. Yet some areas of doctrinal concord also emerged. For instance, mainline early modern Protestants (Lutherans and Reformed) accepted Roman Catholic baptisms. In the same way, Catholics accepted Reformed and Lutheran baptisms. In other words, converts were not re-baptized. A baptism done by an ordained pastor or priest in the name of the Trinity counted. Thus both Catholics and mainline Protestants recognized the validity of each other's baptisms. This mutual recognition sheds new light on toleration issues at the time.

At the local level, communities evolved ways to coexist even in places where one faith was clearly in the majority and had government support. This situation held true in Catholic France and in Lutheran Germany, for instance. These compromises included sharing a church building and holding different worship services for each faith community at different times.

Another strategy was to make some sort of peace with mixed marriages. In France there were couples where one spouse was Catholic and the other was Reformed. These couples came up with creative solutions to deal with their children's religious upbringing. In some cases, the sons were brought up Catholic and the daughters Reformed or vice-versa. Another option was to bring up the first child Reformed, the second Catholic, etc. However, significant points of tension remained. For instance, the religious training of children could become a flashpoint in these mixed marriages. These tensions could become acute particularly if one of the parents died. Relatives on either side might then lay claim to the children to make sure they were brought up in a particular faith.

More generally, conflicts could and did erupt over shared public spaces or community assets. These pressure points included graveyards, the routes of religious processions, and the use of church bells. Yet at the local level in France and elsewhere, Christians showed a creative ability to coexist. These strategies emerged particularly when communities that were divided by faith shared common goals. These goals included economic prosperity and defense against a common enemy. Thus at the local level, rival Christian groups found ways to live together. Coexistence was difficult, but possible.

So people had to figure out how to handle religious pluralism in the early modern era. Official edicts and religious polemic left little room for those who held different beliefs. However, ties of kinship, clan, work, or community could outweigh calls to separate from those holding other beliefs. In our time, tensions are growing between different faiths or worldviews. Let us remember how early modern Christians were sometimes able to see past labels. These examples show how some Christians chose to relate to others in more constructive ways.

FINAL SUMMARY

By 1618, a hundred years after Martin Luther's Ninety-Five Theses, the growth phase of Protestantism in Europe was largely over. So church leaders turned to consolidation. They focused on clear statements of what their group believed and what they rejected. Meanwhile, unresolved political conflicts merged with religious divisions to create a potent mix. In 1618, Europeans began a war that laid parts of the continent to waste for the next thirty years. The causes of the war were both political and religious. In some ways the Thirty Years' War was the end result of the process of division that had begun in 1517.

The early modern European Reformers reframed key theological questions. They reshaped worship and redrew the roles of the laity and the clergy. The state gained new powers over the church. A growing religious pluralism also emerged. This diversity led to debates over how to handle conflicting beliefs or worldviews. At times, early modern Christians came up with creative strategies for religious coexistence. Many of these approaches are worth further thought today. At other times, persecution and the use of force to compel belief prevailed. All western Christians need to acknowledge and repent the mistreatment of religious minority groups and individuals in the name of Christianity during the Reformation.

So does the Reformation still matter in the twenty-first century? Not surprisingly, my answer is *yes*. The early modern experience of divisions in Christian faith and worship was challenging and difficult. Those divisions were then exported and have taken root around the world. We are still living with the legacy of these divisions that have gone on to shape the worldwide church.

But the Reformation still matters today primarily because early modern Christians gained the ability to make a choice about what version of Christianity to follow. They took their faith seriously. Many were willing to risk exile or death. As we saw in Geneva in 1548, men and women could debate what it meant to be a Christian. They came up with very different answers. They looked to different authorities. But the Reformation vastly expanded the range of possible responses and opened the paths for individuals and communities to live out their commitments in new ways.

Notes

Series Editor's Foreword

9 **Midway along the journey of my life:** the opening verse of
The Inferno by Dante Alighieri, trans. Mark Musa (Blooming-
ton and Indianapolis: Indiana University Press, 1995), 19.

10 **We are always on the road:** from Calvin's 34th sermon on
Deuteronomy (5:12-14), preached on June 20, 1555 (*Ioannis
Calvini Opera quae supersunt Omnia*, ed. Johann-Wilhelm
Baum et al. [Brunsvigae: C.A. Schwetschke et Filium, 1883],
26.291), as quoted by Herman Selderhuis (*John Calvin: A
Pilgrim's Life* [Downers Grove, IL: InterVarsity, 2009], 34).

10 **a gift of divine kindness:** from the last chapter of Calvin's
French version of the *Institutes of the Christian Religion*. Titled
"Of the Christian Life," the entire chapter is a guide to wise
and faithful living in this world (*John Calvin, Institutes of the
Christian Religion, 1541 French Edition*, trans. Elsie Anne
McKee [Grand Rapids: Eerdmans, 2009], 704).

Further Reading

The literature on the Reformation is extensive and ever-increasing. Excellent, if lengthy, surveys of the Reformation include Diarmaid MacCulloch, *The Reformation* (New York: Viking, 2004) and Carlos Eire, *Reformations: The Early Modern World, 1450-1650* (New Haven: Yale University Press, 2016). Both of these authors work hard to integrate their narrative within the broader historical and social context and include the Catholic Reformation.

A mid-size and very readable work is Euan Cameron, *The European Reformation,* 2nd ed. (Oxford: Oxford University Press, 2012).

At the other end of the spectrum in terms of length are two very concise accounts of the Reformation and its impact: Patrick Collinson, *The Reformation: A History* (New York: Modern Library, 2004) and Peter Marshall, *The Reformation: A Very Short Introduction* (Oxford: Oxford University Press, 2009).

Some have considered the Reformation and its impact through very specific lenses. For a fascinating study of Luther's use of printing, see Andrew Pettegree, *Brand*

Luther: 1517, Printing, and the Making of the Reformation (New York: Penguin, 2015). Those interested in the Catholic Reformation should see Michael Mullet, *The Catholic Reformation* (London: Routledge, 1999).

Most contemporary scholars tend either to enfold their discussion of the theology of the Reformation within a broader survey of the movement as a whole or to pull out a specific doctrinal issue and examine it in depth. Recent surveys of Reformation theology are thus harder to find. David Bagchi and David Steinmetz, eds, *The Cambridge Companion to Reformation Theology* (Cambridge: Cambridge University Press, 2004) offers a good starting point. Timothy George, *Reading Scripture with the Reformers* (Downers Grove: IVP Academic, 2011) helps in understanding how the Reformers approached the Bible. George's older survey volume, *Theology of the Reformers,* rev. ed., (Nashville: B&H Academic, 2013) considers the theology of each of the leading Reformers in turn. Alister McGrath, *Reformation Thought: an Introduction* 3rd ed. (Malden: Blackwell, 1999) takes a more thematic approach.

There are very few comparative studies of worship in the Reformation era. The essays in Karin Maag and John Witvliet, eds, *Worship in Medieval and Early Modern Worship* (Notre Dame: Notre Dame University Press, 2004) offer good starting points for comparative work. In most cases, scholars have focused on the theology and practice of worship within a given group or in a particular locale. Among the most recent and thorough studies is Elsie Mckee, *The Pastoral Ministry and Worship in Calvin's Geneva* (Geneva: Droz, 2016).

Research on the changing status of the clergy and on church and state issues in the Reformation era has also largely been done on a regional basis. Among the best studies on the clergy in the Reformation era is Amy Nelson Burnett, *Teaching the Reformation: Ministers and Their Message in Basel, 1529-1629* (Oxford: Oxford University Press, 2006). A picture of pastoral ministry in Geneva extending beyond John Calvin's death in 1564 is Scott Manetsch, *Calvin's Company of Pastors: Pastoral Care and the Emerging Reformed Church, 1536-1609* (New York: Oxford University Press, 2013). Fine studies of the complex realm of church-state relations include John Coffey, *Persecution and Toleration in Protestant England, 1558-1689* (Harlow: Longman, 2000), Alexandra Walsham, *Charitable Hatred: Tolerance and Intolerance in England, 1500-1700* (Manchester: Manchester University Press, 2006), and Benjamin Kaplan, *Divided By Faith: Religious Conflict and the Practice of Toleration in Early Modern Europe* (Cambridge, MA: Belknap Press, 2007).

Studies on the long-term impact of the Reformation are growing in number. Thomas Albert Howard and Mark Noll, eds, *Protestantism after 500 Years* (New York: Oxford University Press, 2016) offers a range of essays tying the Reformation to modern issues. Mark Noll and Carolyn Nystrom discuss current relations between Catholics and Protestants in *Is the Reformation Over?* (Grand Rapids: Baker / Bletchley: Pater Noster, 2005). Finally, Brad Gregory, *The Unintended Reformation: How a Religious Revolution Secularized Society* (Cambridge, MA: Belknap Press, 2012), has garnered a great deal of attention and debate over his central thesis highlighted in the title.

Glossary

absenteeism: a clergy member's absence from his duties in a particular location, often as a result of holding several jobs at the same time. Absentee clergy usually paid for someone to cover their duties, albeit at a lower cost.

Act of Six Articles: theological declaration prepared by King **Henry VIII** of England, enacted in 1539. It reaffirmed traditional Catholic doctrines and practices, including the sacrament of confession and prayers to the Virgin Mary.

Anabaptists: an umbrella term for a varied group of sixteenth-century Christians who agreed on the necessity of believers' or adult baptism and rejected infant baptism. Most but not all adopted a pacifist stance and rejected any use of legal oaths. They lacked state support in Western Europe and were heavily persecuted by other Christians.

anointing: putting **consecrated** oil on a person as a mark of blessing.

Apostles' Creed: early Christian statement of faith.

Aquinas, Thomas (1225–1274): medieval Catholic theologian and philosopher whose work helped shape Catholic theological thought.

Augustine of Hippo (354–430): North African theologian and one of the leading fathers of the early Christian church.

Augustinian friars: Catholic religious order established in the thirteenth century.

ban: Among **Anabaptists**, the ban was a form of church discipline by which unrepentant sinners were barred from interactions with their faith community until they repented and were reinstated into the group.

Beza, Theodore (1519–1605): French **Reformed** theologian who spent most of his adult life in **Geneva**. He succeeded **John Calvin** as the leading pastor of Geneva at the latter's death in 1564.

Bohemia: Eastern European kingdom in the sixteenth century, now part of the Czech Republic. **Jan Hus** and the **Hussites** were Bohemian. A conflict over the succession to the crown of Bohemia also launched the **Thirty Years' War**.

Book of Common Prayer: prayer book first published in England in 1549 to provide **liturgies** and directions for worship in the Church of England under **Edward VI**. One of its main authors was Thomas Cranmer, the Archbishop of Canterbury.

Books of Hours: Catholic prayer books for lay people that provided the key texts for the seven daily monastic worship services. The texts included Psalms and prayers. Books of hours could be very plain or beautifully illustrated.

Brandenburg: duchy in the north east of the **Holy Roman Empire**. Brandenburg became Lutheran in 1539.

Bullinger, Heinrich (1504–1575): Swiss theologian and church leader who succeeded **Huldrych Zwingli** as the chief pastor of the **Reformed** church in **Zurich**.

Calvin, John (1509–1564): French theologian and church leader who spent most of his adult life in **Geneva** where he served as the lead pastor from 1541 onwards. He wrote commentaries on nearly every book of the Bible, preached extensively, and maintained a wide network of correspondents.

catechisms: texts designed to teach the basics of Christianity, often through a question and answer format. Among Protestants, Reformation-era catechisms primarily focused on teaching and explaining the Lord's Prayer, the Ten Commandments, and the **Apostles' Creed**.

chantry priests: Catholic clergy whose main duty was to celebrate **Masses** in memory of people who had died. Their income came mainly through gifts from relatives or endowments set up to have these Masses celebrated on a regular basis.

Communion: key Christian sacrament instituted by Jesus Christ at the Last Supper before the crucifixion. Reformation-era Christians divided sharply on the meaning and form of this sacrament.

consecrated: something or someone holy and dedicated to God. Consecration usually involves a ritual of blessing.

consistory: committee of pastors and **elders** in **Reformed** churches charged with church discipline. Their mandate was to ensure that believers lived lives that reflected their faith commitments and to see to it that members of the community of faith lived together as harmoniously as possible. The consistory dealt with family quarrels, marriage matters, neighbor disputes, and issues of faith and behavior. In many Reformed areas, consistories had the authority to bar people from participating in the **Lord's Supper** until their issues had been resolved.

Constance, Council of: Catholic Church council that met from 1414 to 1418. Among other issues, it tried **Jan Hus**, found him guilty of heresy, and had him executed.

Coverdale, Miles (1488–1569): English clergyman and Bible translator, best known for his work on the 1535 English Bible and the Great Bible of 1539.

deaconesses: In his sermons and commentaries, **John Calvin** noted with approval the New Testament model of having faithful Christian widows provide charitable assistance to poor or sick women in the church. These widows were the deaconesses. However, the idea never became a reality in Reformation **Geneva**.

deacons: In the medieval Catholic Church, deacons served as assistants to priests during the **liturgy**. In many cases, deacons were men on the path to the priesthood. In the **Reformed** church during the sixteenth century, deacons could still take on some worship-related duties, but the bulk of their responsibilities involved collecting offerings from church members and caring for the poor and the sick.

Dominicans: members of the Catholic religious order founded by Saint Dominic, established in 1216. In the **early modern** period, Dominicans were primarily known for their preaching, teaching, and missionary work.

Dutch Republic: country in northern Europe made up of seven provinces which had previously been part of the Low Countries under the Catholic rule of the Habsburgs. In 1581, these seven provinces unilaterally declared their independence from Habsburg control. The state church of the Dutch Republic was **Reformed**.

early modern: Historians use this term to refer to the period beginning around 1450, overlapping with the late medieval period. Most historians end the early modern era around 1700 or 1750. On this end, the early modern era overlaps with the **Enlightenment** era.

Edict of Nantes: French document issued by King **Henri IV** in 1598 that gave limited rights to French Protestants, including restricted rights to public worship (not in or near Paris, for instance), access to any profession, and places of safety in case of conflict with Catholic forces. One of the most important features of the edict was the creation of special law courts with equal numbers of Catholic and Protestant judges to settle cases between Catholics and Protestants. The edict put an official end to over thirty years of religious wars in France.

Edward VI (1537-1553): son of **Henry VIII** of England and his third wife, Jane Seymour. He succeeded his father at Henry's death in 1547. Because he was only nine years old at his accession, a regency council ran his government. His advisors' strong Protestantism shaped the young king's outlook and pushed England towards Protestantism. The **Book of Common Prayer** began to shape worship in England beginning in 1549. Edward died at age sixteen and was succeeded by his Catholic half-sister, **Mary I.**

elders: In **Reformed** churches in the sixteenth century, elders were laymen who served alongside pastors to provide spiritual leadership for congregations. Along with the pastors, they served on the **consistory** and helped provide spiritual and moral oversight for the faith community.

elect, the: According to the doctrine of **predestination**, God could rightfully condemn all of humanity because of its sinful condition. According to the Reformers, no one could merit or help achieve their salvation through their deeds. Everyone sinned, and no one could escape the consequences of that sin by their own efforts. Yet God in mercy decided to save some, granting them faith in Christ as their savior. These were the elect. Profound thankfulness, rather than a smug sense of moral superiority, was meant to be the appropriate response. The latter, however, was often prevalent.

Elizabeth I (1533-1603): daughter of **Henry VIII** of England and his second wife, Anne Boleyn. She succeeded her siblings **Edward VI** and **Mary I** to become queen of England in 1558. Under her rule, England followed a middle-of-the-road form of Protestantism, retaining many elements of Catholic worship practices but moving to a **Reformed** theological outlook.

Enlightenment, the: intellectual movement in Europe in the late seventeenth and early eighteenth centuries that emphasized independent thought, free from the restrictions of traditional authorities such as the church. Leading Enlightenment centers included Paris and Edinburgh. Enlightenment thinkers held a generally optimistic view of human possibilities. They valued reason, toleration, and intellectual freedom.

Erasmus of Rotterdam (1466-1536): Dutch humanist and leading European intellectual figure of the sixteenth century. Erasmus' edition of the New Testament in Greek and in a new Latin translation in 1516 decisively shaped Reformation biblical scholarship. To the disappointment of many early Protestants, he remained a faithful Catholic throughout his life, though he shared many of the Reformers' critiques of corruption within the Catholic Church.

exorcism: religious ritual designed to remove the power of the devil from a person or a location.

Frederick the Wise (1463–1525): ruler of **Saxony** from 1486 until his death. He was one of the seven electors who selected the person who would serve as ruler of the **Holy Roman Empire**. Frederick protected **Martin Luther** from the emperor and leaders of the Catholic Church who condemned Luther for heresy. In spite of his defense of Luther, Frederick the Wise remained a Catholic throughout his life, and owned one of Europe's largest collections of relics.

frescoes: images painted on plaster walls. Frescoes in churches often depict biblical scenes, including events from the life of Christ.

friars: male members of Catholic orders dedicated to working among lay people. Some focus on caring for the poor and the sick, while others concentrate on preaching and teaching. Like **monks** and **nuns**, friars take vows of poverty, chastity, and obedience. Franciscans and **Dominicans** are examples of friars.

Froment, Antoine (1508–1581): French **Reformed** preacher and pastor best known for his early work in preaching the message of the Reformation in **Geneva**.

Geneva: In the sixteenth century, Geneva was a town of about 10,000 people. It was originally part of the Duchy of Savoy. But when the city accepted the Reformation in 1535–36, it also split from its political overlord. The newly independent city needed the help of its Protestant neighbors to survive. It took at least a generation before Genevans fully adopted **Reformed** worship and theology.

Genevan Psalter: see Psalter, Genevan

Goodman, Christopher (1520–1603): English Protestant theologian and activist. He studied and taught at Oxford University. When the Catholic queen **Mary I** came to the throne, Goodman went into exile on the European continent. He advocated forceful resistance by ordinary Protestants against their Catholic rulers.

Guise, Charles de (1524–1574): Member of one of the most powerful Catholic noble families in France. He entered the church at a young age and became an archbishop at age fourteen. He became a cardinal in 1547. He served as advisor and diplomat for successive French kings.

Henri II (1551-1589): He was the last of the Valois kings of France. He came to the throne in 1574. He lost the support of the ultra-Catholic party in France, and when he died at the hands of an assassin in 1589, he was succeeded by his Protestant cousin, Henri of Navarre, who became **Henri IV**.

Henri IV (1553-1610): He inherited the small territory of Navarre, on the border between France and Spain, in 1572. He was brought up as a **Reformed** Protestant. In 1572, he married the Catholic Marguerite de Valois, sister of the king of France. A few days after the wedding, the **Saint**

Bartholomew's Day Massacre took place, and Henri was forced to convert to Catholicism. After escaping from the royal court in 1576, he returned to the Reformed faith. Following the death of the last Valois king, **Henri III**, he became king but could not gain the allegiance of the ultra-Catholics in France until he converted once again to Catholicism in 1593. He was assassinated in 1610.

Henry VIII (1491-1547): Henry succeeded to the throne of England in 1509, following his father's death. His inability to produce any living male heirs with his first wife, Catherine of Aragon, led to a dynastic crisis. Ultimately, Henry's advisors engineered a break with the Catholic Church which had refused to dissolve the marriage. In the end, Henry married six times and produced three children: a son **Edward** and daughters **Mary** and **Elizabeth**. In spite of the break with Rome, Henry remained a Catholic in his theology and worship, and England did not see much change in beliefs or religious practice during his lifetime. He was succeeded by his son.

heretic: a person whose beliefs are condemned by others within the same faith group, and who refuses to change these beliefs even when given the opportunity to do so. An accusation of heresy was and is a serious matter, usually involving sharply differing views on key doctrines such as the person of Christ, the nature of God, or the meaning of the sacraments.

Holy Roman Empire: political unit covering much of the central part of Western Europe, from the French border in the west to the border with Poland in the east, and from the North Sea in the north to the Italian city states in the south. The Holy Roman emperor was an elective position: seven leading churchmen and princes in the empire served as the electors. During the Reformation period, each successive emperor came from the Habsburg family.

Hubmaier, Balthasar (1480–1528): **Anabaptist** theologian and church leader. Born in Bavaria, Hubmaier became attracted to Anabaptist ideas, especially adult or believers' baptism, beginning in the early 1520s during his time in **Zurich**. He was forced to recant his views and was exiled from Zurich in 1526. He was executed by Catholic authorities in Vienna in 1528. Hubmaier was one of only a small number of Anabaptists who articulated their theology in writing, and he engaged in an extensive debate with **Huldrych Zwingli** over baptism.

Huguenots: name given to French Protestants who adopted the **Reformed** faith. The origins of the word are debated. The movement grew in popularity in the 1550s and 1560s, reaching its high point around 1562, when about ten percent of France's population adopted the Reformed faith.

humanism: a key intellectual movement of the fifteenth and sixteenth centuries, characterized by a desire to return to the sources of ancient classical learning that flourished in Greece and Rome. Nearly all **early modern** humanists were Christians. They also worked to prepare new editions and translations of the Bible based on the earliest available Hebrew and Greek manuscripts.

Hus, Jan (1369–1415): Born and brought up in **Bohemia**, Jan Hus served as a Catholic priest and popular preacher in Prague. He criticized many of the corrupt practices of the church of his day and supported many of the ideas of **John Wycliffe**. Hus also translated parts of the Englishman's work into Czech. Hus attended the **Council of Constance** under a safe-conduct provided by the Holy Roman emperor. However, Catholic Church leaders had him arrested and charged with heresy. He was executed in July 1415.

Hussites: followers of **Jan Hus** in **Bohemia**. The Hussites called for changes in the beliefs and worship practices of the Catholic Church. After a long struggle involving multiple crusades called against them by the pope, the Hussites achieved one of their main goals, namely the right to receive both the bread and the wine at **Communion**.

iconoclasm: the deliberate destruction of religious images. In the sixteenth century, there were three main reasons why iconoclasts usually attacked religious images. First, iconoclasts were convinced these images encouraged a form of idolatry. Second, iconoclasts felt the images deceived the population because of their supposed spiritual power. Third, the images were targeted because they were a symbol of the church's worldly wealth. At times, individuals destroyed images and statues in riots. At other points, civil authorities systematically removed religious images from church buildings and other public places as a preventative measure to limit violent attacks.

Knox, John (1514–1572): Scottish Reformer and church leader. Knox joined the movement for religious change in Scotland in the 1540s but spent most of the 1550s in exile. He was very much inspired by his experiences in **Calvin's Geneva**. In 1559, Knox returned to Scotland and played a major role in making Scotland Protestant through his leadership and preaching.

liturgy: refers to the order of worship when believers gather together. A liturgy usually involves statements of faith, praise, thanksgiving, confession, petition, and blessing. Churches with strong liturgical practices tend to have a set pattern of worship and may use specific prayers or responses repeatedly.

Lollards: English followers of the ideas of **John Wycliffe**, especially in the fourteenth and fifteenth centuries. Lollards were known for memorizing and reciting large portions of Scripture and condemned the wealth and worldly power of the Catholic Church of their day. By the fifteenth century, they risked being labeled as **heretics** and executed in England.

Lord's Supper: see **Communion**. The term is mostly used among **Reformed** Christians

Luther, Martin (1483–1546): German Reformer whose protest against the Catholic practice of selling indulgences began a course of events that led to the breakup of western Christendom. Luther was a Catholic priest and **Augustinian friar**, and taught at the University of Wittenberg. His study of the New Testament radically reshaped his theology — he began to believe and teach that salvation was a gift of God through divine grace to believers and received by faith, not something that had to be earned. Luther's increasing rejection of papal authority led to his excommunication and condemnation as a **heretic** in 1521. He was an excellent communicator and was proficient at making use of printing to circulate his ideas. Protected by his prince, **Frederick the Wise**, Luther continued to spearhead the Reformation in **Saxony** until his death.

Lutherans: name given to colleagues and followers of Martin Luther from the 1520s onward. The Lutheran church became particularly strong in the **Holy Roman Empire** and in Scandinavia. Lutherans rejected the authority of the Catholic church hierarchy, especially the Pope. They taught that Christ was truly present in the bread and wine at Communion. Compared to the **Reformed** and the **Anabaptists**, the Lutherans retained more aspects of Catholic worship, liturgy, and church government.

Mary I (1516–1558): Mary succeeded her half-brother **Edward VI** on the throne of England in 1553. A lifelong devout Catholic, she worked to bring England back to the Catholic fold. During her reign, nearly three hundred people were executed in England for their Protestant convictions. Mary's marriage to the Catholic Philip II of Spain was viewed with suspicion by many in England. At her death, Mary was succeeded by her half-sister, **Elizabeth I**, who brought England back to Protestantism.

Mass: the central worship service of the Catholic Church. During the ritual of **consecration** of the bread and the wine, these elements are believed to become the body and blood of Christ in substance, though their outward form remains unchanged.

Metrical Psalter: See Psalter, metrical

monks: male members of religious orders who follow a rule and live in community in a monastery. Monks, like **nuns** and **friars**, take vows of poverty, chastity, and obedience. Monks are to devote themselves to lives of prayer.

nave: the longer part of a cross-shaped church building, in which the congregation usually remains. The shorter cross-wise part is known as the transept.

Ninety-five Theses: document prepared by **Martin Luther** in October 1517, containing ninety-five different propositions on indulgences for debate. The posting or advance circulation of theses for debate was a standard part of academic practice at the time.

nuns: female members of religious orders. Nuns, like **monks** and **friars**, take vows of poverty, chastity, and obedience.

Olivétan, Pierre Robert (c. 1506–1538): early French Protestant and Bible translator who prepared one of the earliest complete printed translations of the Bible into French in 1535.

Peasants' War: a series of uprisings and battles that took place mainly in the southern parts of the Holy Roman Empire in 1524 and 1525. The causes of the conflict were mainly economic, as the peasants resisted what they saw as their landlords' efforts to impose new financial and work burdens on them. However, the peasants also took up many of **Luther**'s ideas about the freedom of a Christian and the priesthood of all believers and backed up many of their demands with biblical references. The main peasant army was crushed at the Battle of Frankenhausen in May 1525.

penance: One of the seven sacraments in the Catholic Church, penance involved a sequence of ritual actions, beginning with confession to a priest. Assuming that the person expressed remorse for his or her sins, the priest would grant sacramental forgiveness. The person would also have to make reparation for the sin. This process of reparation could include anything from reciting specific prayers or giving to charity to going on pilgrimage.

Perrot, Charles (1541–1608): French-born pastor who served parishes in the **Genevan** countryside from 1564 to 1568. He left an account of his work and advice for his successor.

pluralism: This practice involved one member of the clergy holding several different posts in the church at the same time, thus benefiting from the combined incomes. Because of the difficulty in being in more than one place at a time, pluralism usually led to **absenteeism**.

Prayer Book Rebellion: This uprising took place in England in 1549 among populations that did not want to accept the new forms of worship in the Church of England based on the **Book of Common Prayer**. Most of those who protested were Catholic.

predestination: The doctrine of predestination, found in Scripture in Romans 8:28–30, teaches that God chooses those whom he saves by granting them faith in Jesus Christ.

Psalter, Genevan: collection of versified Psalms set to music. The entire collection of one hundred and fifty Psalms was available by the early 1560s. Psalm singing became a hallmark of the **Genevan** Reformation, and the practice was exported to other **Reformed** areas around Europe and eventually to North America.

Psalter, metrical (versified): In order to be able to sing the Psalms, they had to be versified or set into meter. The most common practice was to adapt each Psalm so the lines were the same length and rhymed, often in pairs. These practices made the Psalms both easier to sing and easier to remember.

radical Reformation: Scholars have used this umbrella term to refer to groups whose key common characteristic was that they were not mainline Protestant groups (like the **Lutherans** or the **Reformed**). Historians have included the **Anabaptists**, Spiritualists, and Anti-trinitarians among others in this broad category. In most instances, these groups did not garner much political support or protection.

Reformed: In **early modern** Europe, the Reformed were Christians who followed the teachings and practices of the Swiss and **Genevan** churches. The characteristics of the Reformed faith included a vigorous emphasis on Scripture and on preaching, a simple worship style and worship space, and a strong commitment to church discipline.

reprobate, the: According to the doctrine of **predestination**, God could rightfully condemn all of humanity because of its sinful condition. According to the Reformers, no one could merit or help achieve their salvation through their deeds. Everyone sinned, and no one could escape the consequences of that sin by their own efforts. In the working out of this doctrine, the reprobate are those who are not saved by God and are not among **the elect**.

Rousseau, Jean-Jacques (1712-1778): Born in Geneva, Rousseau rebelled against his Reformed upbringing and moved to France as a young man, gaining fame for his philosophical writings, especially his reflections on human society and education. His most famous works include *The Social Contract* (1762) and his *Confessions*, published after his death in 1782.

Saint Andrews: a town on the east coast of Scotland, north of Edinburgh, home of Scotland's first university founded in the 1400s. In the Middle Ages, Saint Andrews was an archbishopric and a place of pilgrimage. Pilgrims came to venerate the relics of Saint Andrew, one of the twelve apostles.

Saint Bartholomew's Day Massacre: an attack by French Catholics against French Protestants that took place in August 1572. The massacre began in Paris following the wedding of Marguerite de Valois, the king's sister, and Henri de Navarre, the leading French Protestant prince (later **Henri IV**). The spate of killings then spread to other French cities.

Saxony: duchy in the northeast of the Holy Roman Empire, home of the University of Wittenberg. **Luther** spent much of his adult working life in Saxony and was protected by its dukes. The Duke of Saxony was one of the seven electors of the Holy Roman emperor.

scientific revolution: intellectual movement in the seventeenth and eighteenth centuries that gave greater weight to observation and experimentation than to reliance on the teachings of previous generations of thinkers.

Sigismund, John, Duke of Brandenburg (1572–1619): ruler of **Brandenburg** beginning in 1608. Although his territory was Lutheran, John Sigismund adopted **Reformed** Protestantism after his studies in Heidelberg. His people (and his Lutheran wife) largely opposed his move to the Reformed faith.

simony: the purchasing of positions in the church, either outright or as a result of a gift given to the church. The word comes from the account of the apostles' encounter with Simon the magician in Acts 8:9–24. He wanted to purchase from them the power to lay hands on believers and enable them to receive the Holy Spirit.

Thirty Years' War: a Europe-wide conflict that ran from 1618 to 1648, with some offshoot conflicts running into the 1650s. Warfare engulfed much of the Holy Roman Empire and led to widespread disruption, violence, and death. The causes of the war included political conflicts between leaders but also unresolved religious tensions emerging from the Reformation era.

tithe: payment in money or in kind made by lay people to the church to help support its clergy and work. Paying the tithe was pretty much compulsory in medieval Europe, and the practice continued in most Protestant areas following the Reformation, though then the tithe was paid to the government who redistributed the income in the form of salaries to pastors.

Twelve Articles of the Peasants: document produced in 1525 by the leaders of the peasant uprisings in the Holy Roman Empire and their supporters. Although these articles dealt primarily with the peasants' grievances against their landowners, the peasants' demands were buttressed by quotations from Scripture. They also called for the right to select their own pastors.

Tyndale, William (c.1494–1536): English Protestant Reformer and Bible translator. He did most of his work translating the Bible outside of England. Catholic authorities eventually arrested him, tried him for heresy, and had him executed.

vernacular: a person's native or mother tongue. In the sixteenth century, Latin was the international language of education and of worship in the Catholic Church. One of the Reformation's major changes was to use the vernacular in worship, though the choice to use one particular language such as English or French still caused difficulties for those who spoke a variant dialect or regional language.

vestments: special garments worn by clergy during worship services. These could range from a simple robe with a stole around the neck to multi-part outfits that were color-coded to match the appropriate **liturgical** season (purple for Lent, red for Pentecost, etc.)

visitations: official visits by clergy and other church leaders to individuals or parishes, designed to check on doctrine, worship, and lifestyle. For instance, visitation committees checked on children's knowledge of the **catechism** and on pastors' performance of their duties.

Weber, Max (1864–1920): German sociologist best known for his thesis that there is a clear affinity between Protestantism (especially in its **Reformed** form) and capitalism.

William of Orange (1533–1584): leading prince and political leader in the **Dutch Republic**. He led the Dutch push for independence from the forces of the Catholic Philip II after 1566, and served as the governor of several of the Dutch provinces from 1572 onwards.

Wishart, George (1513–1546): early Scottish reformer who spread the ideas of **Zwingli** and **Calvin** in Scotland by teaching and preaching. Wishart was executed in 1546 for heresy following a trial conducted by the Scottish Catholic cardinal David Beaton.

Wittenberg: small town in **Saxony** whose claims to fame included the presence of the University of Wittenberg and the teaching and preaching activity of **Martin Luther** and other leading Lutheran theologians and Reformers.

Wycliffe, John (c. 1330–1384): English priest, academic, and theologian who objected to several aspects of church doctrine and practice in his day. In particular, he criticized the church's wealth and worldly power and condemned devotional practices such as pilgrimages and prayers to the saints. Wycliffe also worked on translating parts of the New Testament into English and gave impetus to a complete English translation of the Bible that circulated after his death. Although he faced opposition and investigation for his views, Wycliffe was never condemned as a **heretic** during his lifetime and died of natural causes.

Zurich: Swiss canton and city of the same name in the northeastern Swiss lands. Zurich formally adopted the **Reformed** faith in the 1520s, largely as a result of the preaching and advocacy of **Huldrych Zwingli** and his fellow clergy. Zurich, along with **Geneva**, became a key reference point for Reformed Protestants across Europe.

Zwingli, Huldrych (1484–1531): Swiss Reformer and church leader. Zwingli was a well-educated Catholic priest whose move to Reformation theology was shaped to a large extent by his study of **Erasmus'** Greek New Testament. Zwingli began the process of reform in **Zurich** following his appointment as priest in the city in 1519. By 1525, the **Mass** was banned in Zurich. Conflicts grew between the Protestant Swiss cantons (led by Zurich and Bern) and the Catholic cantons, leading to two wars. In the second battle at Kappel in 1531, Zwingli and several other Zurich pastors were killed.